Easy Learning

Times tables Workbook 3

Age 7-11

Simon Greaves

This book belongs to

How to use this book

- Easy Learning workbooks help your child improve basic skills, build confidence and develop a love of learning.
- Find a quiet, comfortable place to work, away from distractions.
- Get into a routine of completing one or two workbook pages with your child every day.
- Ask your child to circle the star that matches how many questions they have completed every two pages:

Some = half of the questions

Most = more than half

All = all the questions

- The progress certificate at the back of this book will help you and your child keep track of how many ★ have been circled.
- Encourage your child to work through all of the questions eventually, and praise them for completing the progress certificate.
- Each workbook builds on the previous one in the series. Help your child complete this one to ensure they have covered what they need to know before starting the next workbook.

- The ability to recall and use times tables facts is an essential skill and is invaluable for many mathematical processes.
- Learning tables at an early age gives your child confidence with numbers.

Parent tip
Look out for tips on how to help your child learn tables.

Published by Collins
An imprint of HarperCollinsPublishers
77–85 Fulham Palace Road
Hammersmith
London
W6 8JB

Browse the complete Collins catalogue at
www.collinseducation.com

First published in 2011
© HarperCollinsPublishers 2011

10 9 8 7 6 5 4 3 2 1

ISBN-13 978-0-00-744984-2

The author asserts the moral right to be identified as the author of this work.

British Library Cataloguing in Publication Data
A catalogue record for this publication is available from the British Library

Written by Simon Greaves
Design and layout by Linda Miles, Lodestone Publishing
Illustrated by Graham Smith
Cover design by Linda Miles
Cover illustration by Graham Smith
Packaged and project managed by White-Thomson Publishing Ltd
Printed and bound by Martins the Printers, Berwick Upon Tweed

Contents

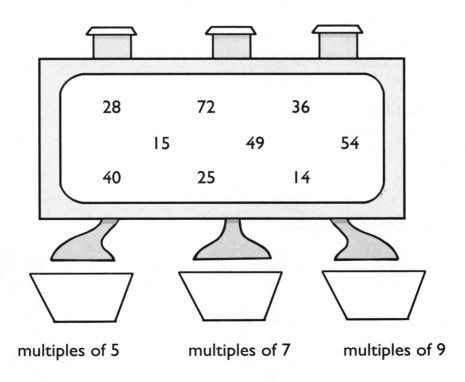

28   72   36
   15   49   54
40   25   14

multiples of 5   multiples of 7   multiples of 9

Odd tables

1 For each pyramid, work out the answer in each circle.
Colour yellow the circle with the highest answer.
Colour purple the circle with the lowest answer.

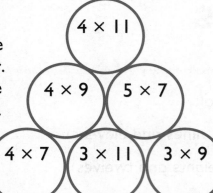
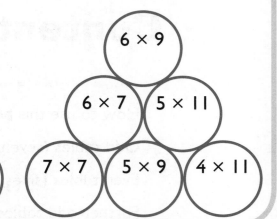

2 Fill in the answers on the multiplication steps.

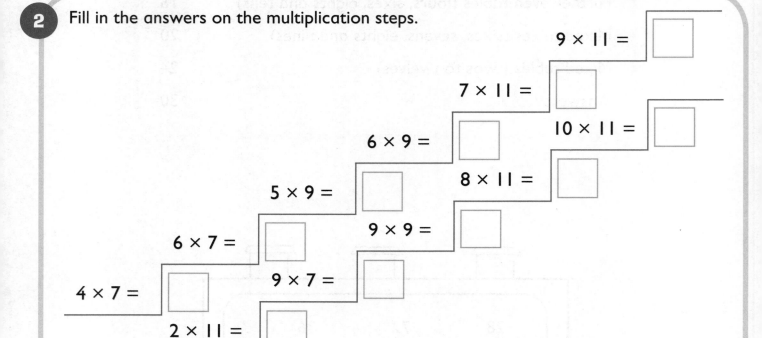

$9 \times 11 =$

$7 \times 11 =$

$10 \times 11 =$

$6 \times 9 =$

$8 \times 11 =$

$5 \times 9 =$

$9 \times 9 =$

$6 \times 7 =$

$9 \times 7 =$

$4 \times 7 =$

$2 \times 11 =$

$3 \times 7 =$

3 Complete the multiplication grids.

×	7	9
2		
4		
6		

×	7	11
1		
5		
8		

×	9	11
3		
7		
10		

4

4 Find the product of:

3 and 9 ▢

10 and 11 ▢

8 and 9 ▢

7 and 7 ▢

7 and 9 ▢

7 and 11 ▢

Parent tip
Ask your child to write out the full seven, nine and eleven times tables.

5 Here are the ticket prices for entry to a funfair. How much would it cost to buy tickets for:

Adult	£11
Child under 16	£9
Child under 10	£7

9 adults £ ▢

4 children under 16 £ ▢

5 children under 10 £ ▢

How many adult tickets can you buy with £33? ▢

How many tickets for children under 16 can you buy with £54? ▢

6 An archer fires three arrows. He multiplies the number on the arrow by the score on the target. Work out the score for each arrow. Write the scores in the boxes next to each arrow.

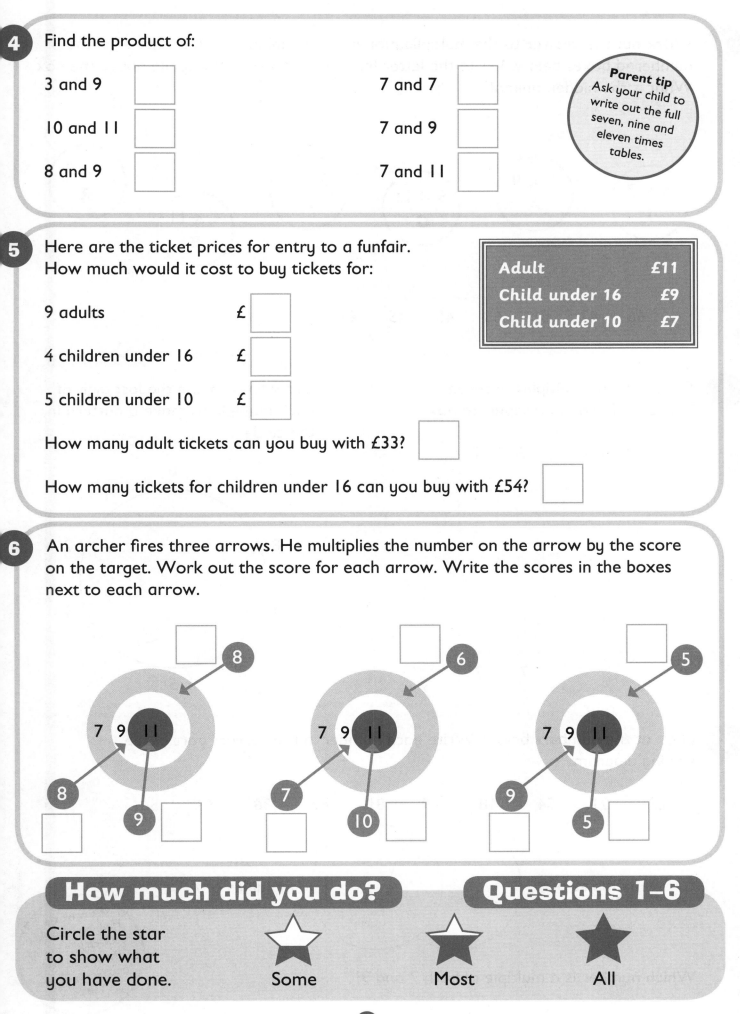

How much did you do?   Questions 1–6

Circle the star to show what you have done.

Some   Most   All

7 Work out the answer to the multiplication in each bubble. Find this answer in the numbered boxes below. Write the letter from that bubble in the space above the box. What is the hidden animal?

_____

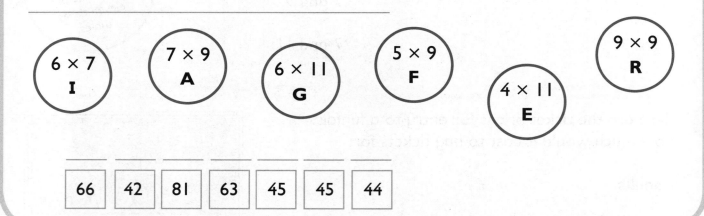

66	42	81	63	45	45	44

8 Complete the multiples of seven. Write each digit in a separate box.

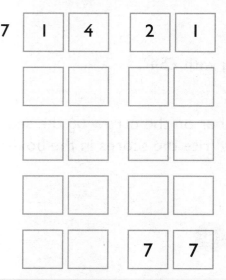

Draw lines to join the last digit of each multiple to make a pattern in the circle.

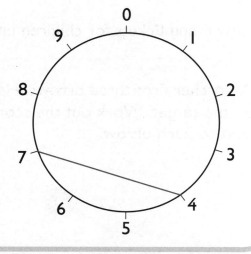

9 Look at the numbers below. Write each number in the correct part of the sorting diagram.

27   21   54   18   49   81   42   36   63   56

multiples of 9   multiples of 7

Which number is a multiple of both 7 and 9? ☐

10 Complete this speed test. Record your score and time taken below the speed test.

$3 \times 11 =$ ⬚ $6 \times 9 =$ ⬚ $4 \times 11 =$ ⬚

$9 \times 7 =$ ⬚ $9 \times 9 =$ ⬚ $4 \times 7 =$ ⬚

$7 \times 11 =$ ⬚ $3 \times 9 =$ ⬚ $10 \times 11 =$ ⬚

$7 \times 7 =$ ⬚ $2 \times 11 =$ ⬚ $6 \times 7 =$ ⬚

$1 \times 11 =$ ⬚ $8 \times 11 =$ ⬚ $6 \times 11 =$ ⬚

$2 \times 7 =$ ⬚ $1 \times 7 =$ ⬚ $2 \times 9 =$ ⬚

$8 \times 9 =$ ⬚ $1 \times 9 =$ ⬚ $7 \times 9 =$ ⬚

$3 \times 7 =$ ⬚ $10 \times 7 =$ ⬚ $5 \times 9 =$ ⬚

$5 \times 11 =$ ⬚ $10 \times 9 =$ ⬚ $8 \times 7 =$ ⬚

$9 \times 11 =$ ⬚ $5 \times 7 =$ ⬚ $4 \times 9 =$ ⬚

SCORE

TIME

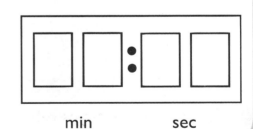

0   10   20   30   min   sec

Even tables

1 Complete the puzzle by finding the answers to the multiplications.

Across	**Down**
2 2 × 6	**1** 9 × 8
3 9 × 12	**2** 10 × 12
5 6 × 6	**3** 2 × 8
6 6 × 8	**4** 7 × 12
	5 4 × 8
	7 10 × 8

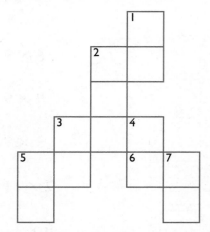

2 Complete the first six multiples of six and eight. Write each digit in a separate box.

6 | 1 | 2 | | | | | | | | | | |

8 | | | | | | | | | | | | |

Draw lines to join the last digit of each multiple to make patterns in the circles.

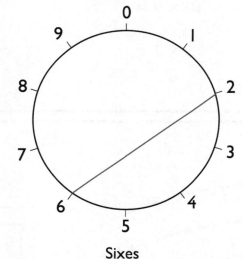

Sixes

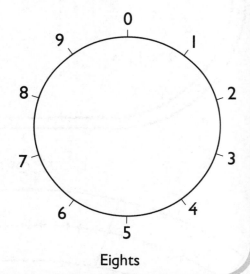

Eights

3 Complete these times tables facts.

☐ × 6 = 18   ☐ × 8 = 24   ☐ × 12 = 120

☐ × 8 = 56   ☐ × 12 = 96   ☐ × 6 = 42

☐ × 12 = 12   ☐ × 6 = 30   ☐ × 8 = 64

4 Here is a number grid. Shade a path from Start to Finish that only goes through multiples of six, eight or twelve.

2	38	17	22	7	9	40	→ Finish
7	14	26	19	36	16	84	
34	18	72	60	24	35	11	
48	42	37	62	79	5	13	
54	9	15	73	77	25	31	
Start → 12	20	3	49	85	4	1	

5 For each number, write different multiplication facts from the six, eight and twelve times tables only.

36

24

48

Parent tip
Help your child to learn the six, eight and twelve times tables by heart.

6 Answer these questions.

What is the product of 9 and 8?

What is the eighth multiple of 12?

What do you need to multiply 6 by to get 42?

Which number multiplied by 12 is 84?

How much did you do?   ## Questions 1–6

Circle the star to show what you have done.

 Some

 Most

 All

7 Use the six, eight and twelve times tables to fill in the missing multiplications and answers in the bricks and make the walls match. The top pair of bricks has been done for you.

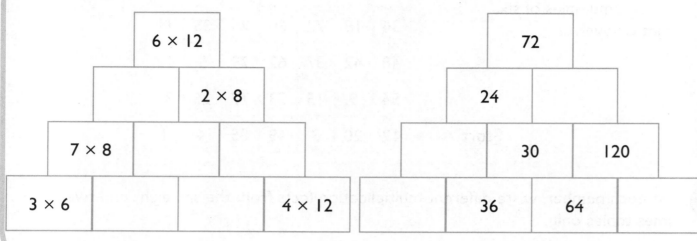

8 Eggs are packed in boxes of different sizes.
How many eggs are there in:

8 small boxes ⬜ | 5 medium boxes ⬜

9 large boxes ⬜ | 4 small boxes ⬜

7 medium boxes ⬜ | 3 large boxes ⬜

Small	6 eggs
Medium	8 eggs
Large	12 eggs

List the ways in which 48 eggs can be packed.

_____

9 Write in the multiples of six, eight and twelve to complete the snakes.

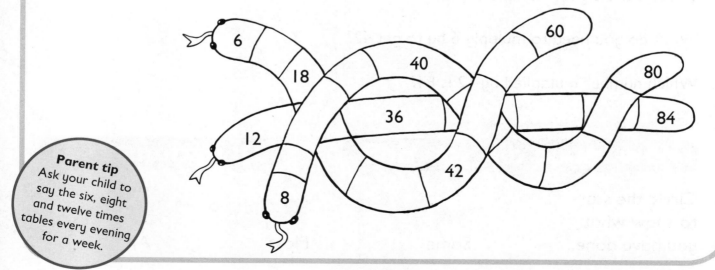

Parent tip
Ask your child to say the six, eight and twelve times tables every evening for a week.

10 Complete this speed test. Record your score and time taken below the speed test.

10 × 6 = ☐

5 × 8 = ☐

4 × 12 = ☐

7 × 8 = ☐

1 × 12 = ☐

2 × 8 = ☐

9 × 12 = ☐

6 × 6 = ☐

9 × 6 = ☐

8 × 6 = ☐

3 × 8 = ☐

5 × 12 = ☐

3 × 12 = ☐

7 × 12 = ☐

9 × 8 = ☐

5 × 6 = ☐

8 × 8 = ☐

4 × 6 = ☐

2 × 6 = ☐

7 × 6 = ☐

6 × 12 = ☐

4 × 8 = ☐

10 × 12 = ☐

6 × 8 = ☐

2 × 12 = ☐

3 × 6 = ☐

8 × 12 = ☐

1 × 8 = ☐

1 × 6 = ☐

10 × 8 = ☐

SCORE

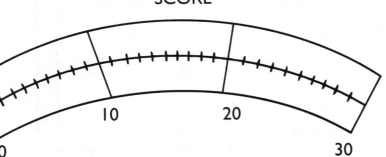

TIME

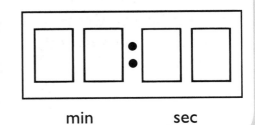

min   sec

How much did you do?   **Questions 7–10**

Circle the star to show what you have done.

Some   Most   All

Further odd tables

1 Work out the answers across and down to complete the puzzles.

(4) × (3) = ☐   (6) × (9) = ☐

×   ×   ×   ×

(9) × (5) = ☐   (7) × (3) = ☐

=   =   =   =

☐   ☐   ☐   ☐

2 Complete the multiplication grid.

Parent tip
Record mixed tables facts on a media player for your child to listen to and repeat.

×	6	9	7	8	4
3					
7					
5					
9					

3 Here is a machine that sorts numbers. Sort the numbers into multiples of five, seven and nine and write them in the correct bucket. Cross out the numbers as you sort them.

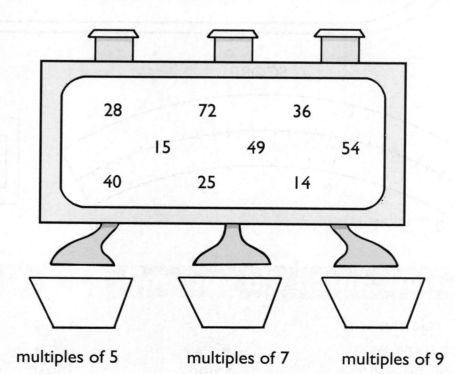

28   72   36
    15   49   54
40   25   14

multiples of 5   multiples of 7   multiples of 9

4 An archer fires three arrows. He multiplies the number on the arrow by the score on the target. Work out the score for each arrow. Write the scores in the boxes next to each arrow.

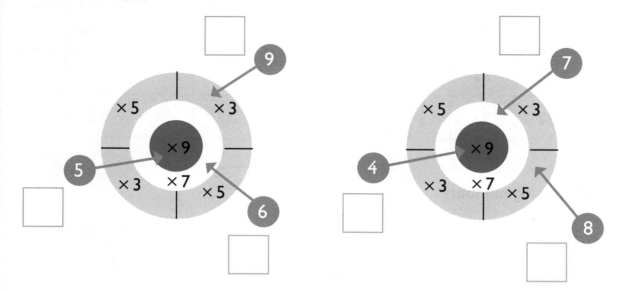

5 Answer these questions.

What are eight sevens? ☐

What is 7 multiplied by 9? ☐

How many nines in 72? ☐

Multiply ten by five. ☐

Find the product of 4 and 3. ☐

Multiply seven by itself. ☐

6 An adult ticket for the cinema costs £8 and a child ticket costs £6. How much would it cost for:

5 adult tickets £ ☐

7 child tickets £ ☐

9 adult tickets £ ☐

3 child tickets £ ☐

Adult £8

Child £6

How much did you do?   Questions 1–6

Circle the star to show what you have done.

 Some

 Most

 All

7 Here is part of a number grid. Write a multiplication from the three, five, seven or nine times table for each of the missing numbers. The first one has been done for you.

11	4 × 3	13			16	17		19	
	22	23			26			29	
31	32	33	34			37	38	39	

8 Fill in the missing numbers.

☐ × 3 = 6   ☐ × 5 = 20   ☐ × 9 = 90

☐ × 7 = 28   ☐ × 3 = 15   ☐ × 7 = 14

☐ × 9 = 54   ☐ × 7 = 56   ☐ × 3 = 24

☐ × 5 = 5   ☐ × 9 = 36   ☐ × 5 = 50

9 Colour the picture using the code key below.

Code key
answers in the 3 times table
= brown
answers in the 5 times table
= blue
answers in the 7 times table
= yellow
answers in the 9 times table
= green

Parent tip
Take turns to recite alternate three, five, seven and nine times tables facts with your child.

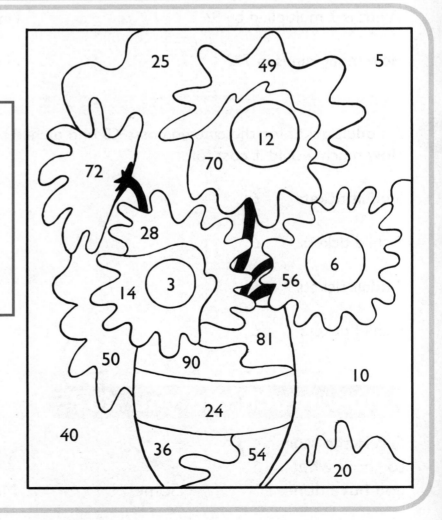

10 Complete this speed test. Record your score and time taken below the speed test.

2 × 5 =	4 × 7 =	9 × 7 =
10 × 9 =	10 × 7 =	6 × 3 =
5 × 9 =	3 × 9 =	3 × 7 =
7 × 7 =	6 × 9 =	7 × 5 =
1 × 5 =	2 × 9 =	9 × 5 =
7 × 3 =	8 × 5 =	1 × 9 =
1 × 3 =	2 × 3 =	2 × 7 =
9 × 3 =	8 × 3 =	6 × 7 =
7 × 9 =	1 × 7 =	3 × 5 =
10 × 5 =	8 × 9 =	6 × 5 =

SCORE

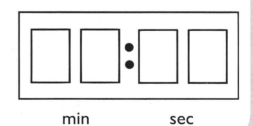

0   10   20   30

TIME

min   sec

Further even tables

1 For each triangle, colour red the part with the highest answer. Colour blue the part with the lowest answer.

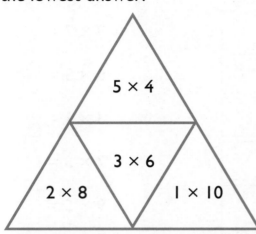

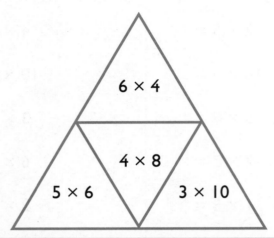

2 Complete the multiplication grids.

×	7	2
8		
4		

×	3	5
8		
10		

×		
6	36	
8		72

3 Complete the multiplication steps.

9 × 6 = ☐

4 × 8 = ☐

9 × 8 = ☐

5 × 6 = ☐

6 × 10 = ☐

7 × 4 = ☐

5 × 8 = ☐

3 × 8 = ☐

6 × 6 = ☐

2 × 10 = ☐

6 × 4 = ☐

3 × 4 = ☐

4 Fill in the missing numbers.

☐ × 4 = 12   ☐ × 6 = 24   ☐ × 8 = 40

☐ × 10 = 60   ☐ × 6 = 42   ☐ × 4 = 32

☐ × 10 = 20   ☐ × 8 = 64   ☐ × 10 = 50

☐ × 8 = 16   ☐ × 6 = 36   ☐ × 4 = 20

5 Work out the answers to each multiplication. Use the answers to find the correct colour in the code key. Colour the picture.

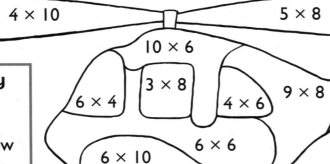

Code key
24 = blue
36 = grey
40 = yellow
54 = black
60 = green
72 = brown

6 Complete the number sequences using multiples of four, six, eight or ten.

18   24   ☐ ☐ ☐ ☐

48   40   ☐ ☐ ☐ ☐

32   28   ☐ ☐ ☐ ☐

☐ ☐   40 ☐   20 ☐

Parent tip
Ask your child to write out the four, six, eight and ten times tables in full.

How much did you do?   **Questions 1–6**

Circle the star to show what you have done.

 Some   Most   All

17

7 Work out the answer to the multiplication in each bubble. Find this answer in the numbered boxes below. Write the letter from that bubble in the space above the box. What is the hidden word?

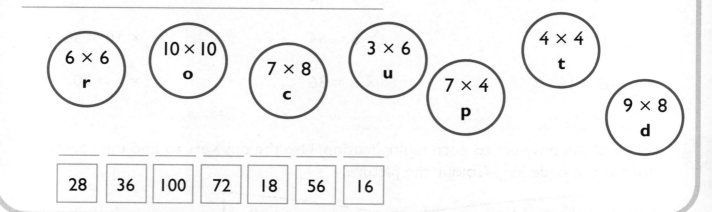

| 28 | 36 | 100 | 72 | 18 | 56 | 16 |

8 In each line, circle the multiplication or multiplications that match the number in the box.

40	9 × 4	7 × 6	4 × 10	5 × 8
12	3 × 4	2 × 8	2 × 10	2 × 6
54	7 × 8	6 × 10	9 × 6	6 × 8
24	6 × 4	4 × 6	3 × 8	3 × 10

Parent tip
Ask your child to make a poster of the four, six, eight and ten times tables to stick on the wall.

9 It costs £10 to hire a taxi. The taxi can carry six people and eight bags.

How much would it cost to hire 3 taxis? £ ☐

How many bags can 7 taxis carry? ☐

How many people can 5 taxis carry? ☐

How many wheels are there on 6 taxis? ☐

A group of 24 people needs to hire taxis.

How many taxis will they need? ☐

How much will it cost? £ ☐

10 Complete this speed test. Record your score and time taken below the speed test.

$4 \times 4 =$ ☐ $8 \times 4 =$ ☐ $10 \times 6 =$ ☐

$9 \times 8 =$ ☐ $9 \times 4 =$ ☐ $4 \times 8 =$ ☐

$7 \times 10 =$ ☐ $8 \times 10 =$ ☐ $8 \times 6 =$ ☐

$7 \times 8 =$ ☐ $4 \times 6 =$ ☐ $6 \times 8 =$ ☐

$3 \times 6 =$ ☐ $6 \times 10 =$ ☐ $7 \times 6 =$ ☐

$2 \times 8 =$ ☐ $1 \times 8 =$ ☐ $7 \times 4 =$ ☐

$2 \times 6 =$ ☐ $9 \times 6 =$ ☐ $6 \times 4 =$ ☐

$3 \times 8 =$ ☐ $10 \times 8 =$ ☐ $5 \times 4 =$ ☐

$6 \times 6 =$ ☐ $10 \times 4 =$ ☐ $5 \times 8 =$ ☐

$9 \times 10 =$ ☐ $8 \times 8 =$ ☐ $5 \times 6 =$ ☐

SCORE

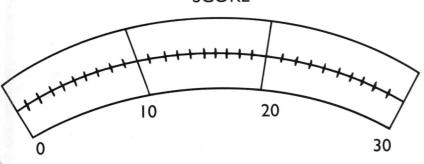

TIME

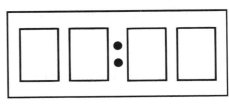

min   sec

How much did you do?   Questions 7–10

Circle the star to show what you have done.

Some

Most

All

Mixed tables

1 This is a recipe to make an ice-cream sundae for one person. Write what you would need to make ice-cream sundaes for:

> 3 scoops of ice cream
>
> 4 spoons of jelly
>
> 6 strawberries

6 people

[ ] scoops of ice cream

[ ] spoons of jelly

[ ] strawberries

7 people

[ ] scoops of ice cream

[ ] spoons of jelly

[ ] strawberries

2 Choose the correct answer for each multiplication. Colour the letter next to that answer. The letters you have **not** coloured spell out a number.

$4 \times 6 = 24$ [t]   or   27 [s]

$6 \times 9 = 56$ [i]   or   54 [w]

$8 \times 8 = 72$ [x]   or   64 [a]

$4 \times 7 = 28$ [s]   or   30 [t]

$5 \times 9 = 40$ [e]   or   45 [l]

$6 \times 6 = 36$ [i]   or   35 [e]

$8 \times 9 = 64$ [n]   or   72 [t]

Parent tip
Quiz your child once a week on the six, seven, eight and nine times tables.

What is the number? _____

3 Answer these questions.

What is the ninth multiple of nine? [ ]

What are four nines? [ ]

How many eights in 64? [ ]

Multiply 9 by eight. [ ]

What number multiplied by 7 is 63? [ ]

The fifth multiple of six is 30. True or false? _____

4 Count on or back to complete each number sequence.

27	36			63		
49	42					7
32	40					80
6				30		

5 Here are the ticket prices for some attractions.

Castle	£6	Funfair	£8
Museum	£7	Zoo	£9

How much would it cost to buy:

Nine funfair tickets £ ☐   Six tickets for the castle £ ☐

Three museum tickets £ ☐   Eight tickets for the zoo £ ☐

How many zoo tickets can you buy with £54? ☐

How many museum tickets can you buy with £42? ☐

6 Look at the numbers in the box.
Circle red the multiples of 6.
Circle green the multiples of 7.
Circle blue the multiples of 9.
Circle black the multiples of 8.

12   27   40
   30   64
42   14
   56   63

Which number has been circled in green and black? ☐

Which number has been circled in green and blue? ☐

Which number has been circled in green and red? ☐

How much did you do?   Questions 1–6

Circle the star to show what you have done.

 Some   Most   All

21

7 Two people are playing times tables bingo. Here are the tables that have been called.

(5 × 6) (6 × 7) (7 × 9) (6 × 9) (9 × 8) (8 × 7) (3 × 9)

Player A

30	42	27
54	72	56

Player B

42	54	72
35	50	63

The player that has the most answers is the winner. Shade the answers on each player's bingo card that match the multiplications.

Who won, Player A or Player B? _____

8 Draw lines to match each multiplication to its answer.

(9 × 6) (7 × 7) (9 × 9) (6 × 8) (7 × 9) (3 × 6)

(81) (18) (49) (63) (54) (48)

9 Find the right route. You can only go along roads with numbers that are answers in the six, seven, eight and nine times tables.

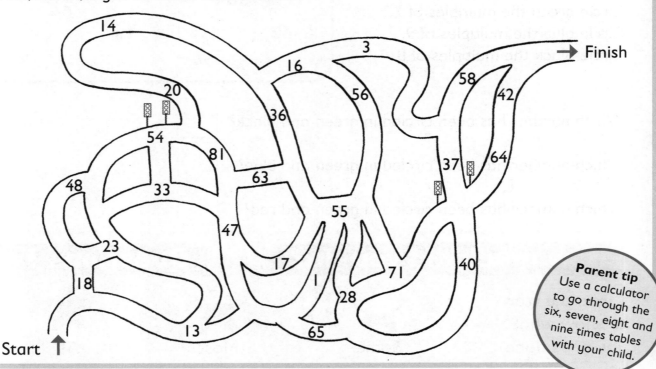

Complete this speed test. Record your score and time taken below the speed test.

4 × 9 = ☐   8 × 9 = ☐   10 × 6 = ☐

9 × 8 = ☐   9 × 9 = ☐   4 × 8 = ☐

7 × 7 = ☐   8 × 7 = ☐   8 × 6 = ☐

7 × 8 = ☐   4 × 7 = ☐   6 × 8 = ☐

3 × 6 = ☐   6 × 7 = ☐   7 × 6 = ☐

2 × 8 = ☐   1 × 8 = ☐   7 × 9 = ☐

5 × 9 = ☐   9 × 6 = ☐   6 × 9 = ☐

3 × 8 = ☐   10 × 8 = ☐   9 × 7 = ☐

6 × 6 = ☐   10 × 9 = ☐   8 × 8 = ☐

10 × 7 = ☐   5 × 8 = ☐   5 × 6 = ☐

SCORE

TIME

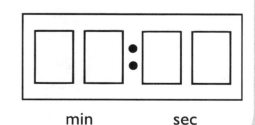

min   sec

How much did you do?   **Questions 7–10**

Circle the star to show what you have done.

Some

Most

All

Mixed tables

1 For each hexagon, colour red the triangle with the highest answer. Colour blue the triangle with the lowest answer.

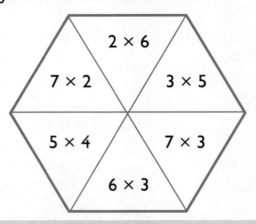
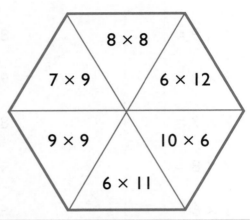

2 Draw lines to match each multiplication to the correct answer.

(9 × 3)　(7 × 11)　(6 × 4)　(7 × 7)　(9 × 8)　(6 × 2)　(8 × 12)

(24)　(49)　(77)　(12)　(27)　(96)　(72)

3 Two numbers that multiply to give another number are called a factor pair.
For example, 5 and 6 and 10 and 3 are both factor pairs of 30.
Complete the factor pairs for the number in the middle.

Parent tip
Use sticky notes to create a mixed tables trail around the house.

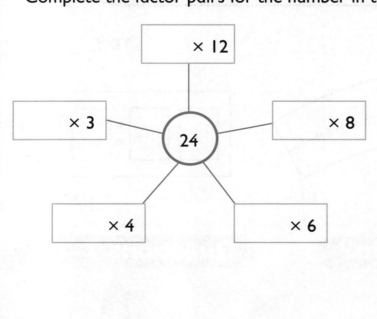
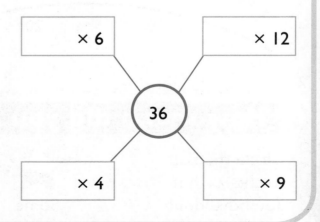

24

4 Complete the multiplication grids.

×	7	9	4
4			
6			
7			

×	8	6	3
8			
3			
12			

×	4	10	
	36		
11			55
		20	

5 Answer these questions.

What are six nines? ☐

What is four multiplied by two? ☐

What is 8 times 7? ☐

What is the product of 9 and 3? ☐

What is the third multiple of 12? ☐

Which number multiplied by 8 is 48? ☐

6 Multiply the number on the arrow by the score on the target. Work out the score for each arrow. Write the score in the box next to each arrow.

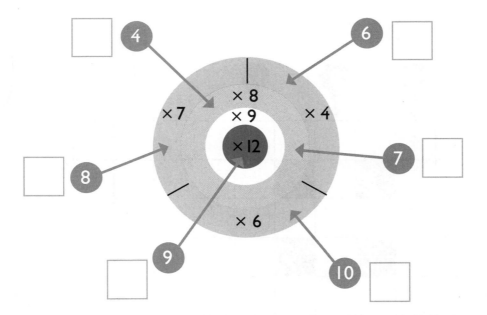

7 Choose two different numbers from the box. Write out the numbers as a multiplication on a piece of paper and then work out the answer. Make as many multiplications as you can.

> 5   7
>   8   4
> 2   9   6

8 Fill in the missing numbers.

☐ × 2 = 18   ☐ × 3 = 24   ☐ × 4 = 36

☐ × 5 = 45   ☐ × 6 = 18   ☐ × 7 = 56

☐ × 8 = 72   ☐ × 9 = 36   ☐ × 9 = 9

☐ × 10 = 50   ☐ × 11 = 99   ☐ × 12 = 24

9 Complete each sequence of multiples to solve the number puzzle.

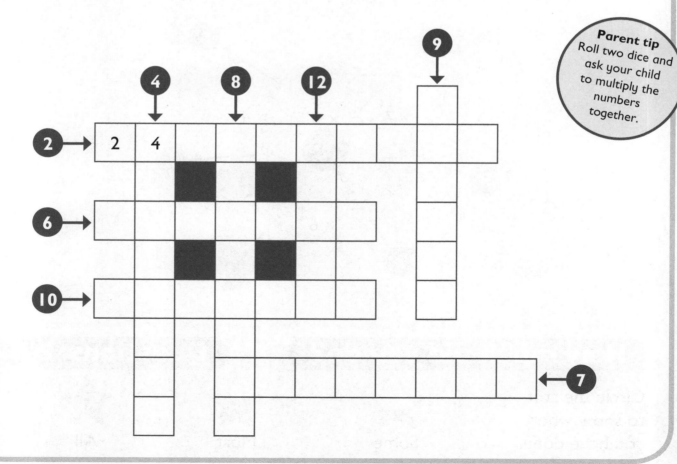

Parent tip
Roll two dice and ask your child to multiply the numbers together.

0 In each line, draw boxes round the multiplications that match the number in the circle.

72   8 × 9   6 × 12   9 × 7   8 × 8

45   4 × 11   5 × 9   7 × 6   9 × 5

60   5 × 12   7 × 9   7 × 8   10 × 6

48   7 × 7   8 × 6   4 × 12   5 × 9

1 Work out the multiplications across and down to complete the puzzles.

8 × 9 = ☐   6 × 7 = ☐

×   ×   ×   ×

4 × 6 = ☐   8 × 7 = ☐

=   =   =   =

☐   ☐   ☐   ☐

2 Use the odd number times tables to fill in the missing multiplications and answers in the bricks and make the walls match. The top pair of bricks has been done for you.

Wall 1:
- 9 × 7
- 8 × 5
- 10 × 11
- 7 × 3 | | 2 × 9 |

Wall 2:
- 63
- 25
- 42 | | 27
- | 72 | | 55

13 Complete the puzzle by finding the answers to the multiplications.

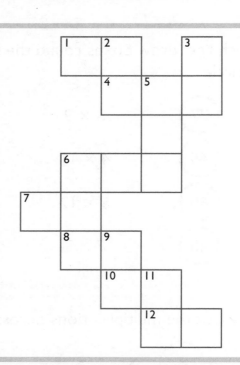

Across	Down
1 9 × 8	**2** 3 × 7
4 10 × 11	**3** 4 × 5
6 10 × 12	**5** 10 × 10
7 6 × 10	**6** 9 × 12
8 9 × 9	**9** 4 × 4
10 8 × 8	**11** 4 × 11
12 8 × 6	

---

14 Here are some multiplications. Some are correct and some are not.
Put a tick next to those with the correct answer. ✔
Put a cross next to those with the wrong answer. ✘

8 × 7 = 56 ☐   7 × 3 = 24 ☐

7 × 6 = 48 ☐   8 × 4 = 32 ☐

8 × 9 = 74 ☐   5 × 8 = 42 ☐

6 × 12 = 72 ☐   9 × 11 = 99 ☐

Parent tip
Use the progress certificate at the back of this book to make a reward chart for your child.

---

15 Fill in the missing numbers in the number machine.

× 12

☐ → 48
☐ → 108
☐ → 24
☐ → 96
☐ → 36

6 Complete the ultimate tables test. Record your score and time below.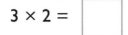

3 × 2 = ☐	4 × 12 = ☐	7 × 5 = ☐
6 × 3 = ☐	2 × 12 = ☐	7 × 12 = ☐
7 × 2 = ☐	5 × 3 = ☐	10 × 2 = ☐
9 × 4 = ☐	9 × 2 = ☐	4 × 8 = ☐
5 × 4 = ☐	5 × 11 = ☐	1 × 11 = ☐
3 × 4 = ☐	2 × 7 = ☐	2 × 9 = ☐
5 × 6 = ☐	7 × 3 = ☐	9 × 11 = ☐
8 × 6 = ☐	9 × 10 = ☐	10 × 9 = ☐
6 × 6 = ☐	6 × 9 = ☐	6 × 10 = ☐
6 × 8 = ☐	1 × 4 = ☐	4 × 2 = ☐
9 × 5 = ☐	8 × 9 = ☐	10 × 5 = ☐
9 × 7 = ☐	8 × 7 = ☐	2 × 11 = ☐
4 × 9 = ☐	6 × 7 = ☐	7 × 4 = ☐
8 × 10 = ☐	3 × 6 = ☐	9 × 3 = ☐
9 × 8 = ☐	3 × 5 = ☐	6 × 2 = ☐
9 × 12 = ☐	3 × 3 = ☐	4 × 7 = ☐

SCORE

0   24   48

TIME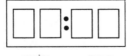

min   sec

41–48	Outstanding!
33–40	Very good
25–32	Getting there
24 or less	Have another go!

How much did you do?

Questions 13–16

Circle the star to show what you have done.

 Some

 Most

 All

29

Answers

Odd tables (sevens, nines and elevens)

Page 4

1   4 × 11 – yellow, 3 × 9 – purple;
    5 × 11 – yellow, 6 × 7 – purple

2   28, 42, 45, 54, 77, 99; 21, 22, 63, 81, 88, 110

3   First grid ×7 – 14, 28, 42; ×9 – 18, 36, 54;
    second grid ×7 – 7, 35, 56; ×11 – 11, 55, 88;
    third grid ×9 – 27, 63, 90; ×11 – 33, 77, 110

Page 5

4   27, 49, 110, 63, 72, 77

5   £99, £36, £35, 3, 6

6   (Clockwise from top) 56, 99, 72; 42, 110,
    63; 35, 55, 81

Page 6

7   Giraffe

8   28, 35, 42, 49, 56, 63, 70

9   Multiples of 9 – 27, 54, 18, 81, 36, 63;
    multiples of 7 – 21, 49, 42, 56, 63; 63

Page 7

10 33, 54, 44, 63, 81, 28, 77, 27, 110, 49, 22,
    42, 11, 88, 66, 14, 7, 18, 72, 9, 63, 21, 70,
    45, 55, 90, 56, 99, 35, 36

Even tables (sixes, eights and twelves)

Page 8

1   Across – (2) 12, (3) 108, (5) 36, (6) 48;
    down – (1) 72, (2) 120, (3) 16, (4) 84,
    (5) 32, (7) 80

2   (6), (12), 18, 24, 30, 36; (8), 16, 24, 32,
    40, 48

3   3, 3, 10, 7, 8, 7, 1, 5, 8

Page 9

4   Start, 12, 54, 48, 42, 18, 72, 60, 24, 36, 16,
    84, 40, Finish

5   6 × 6, 3 × 12; 4 × 6, 3 × 8, 2 × 12; 8 × 6,
    6 × 8, 4 × 12

6   72, 96, 7, 7

Page 10

7   First wall (from top) – 4 × 6 or 3 × 8 or 2
    × 12, 5 × 6, 10 × 12, 6 × 6 or 3 × 12, 8 ×
    8; second wall (from top) – 16, 56, 18, 48

8   48, 40, 108, 24, 56, 36; 8 small boxes,
    6 medium boxes and 4 large boxes

9   6 – 12, 24, 30, 36, 48, 54; 8 – 16, 24, 32,
    48, 56, 64, 72; 12 – 24, 48, 60, 72

Page 11

10 60, 24, 72, 40, 60, 32, 48, 36, 120, 56, 84,
    48, 12, 72, 24, 16, 30, 18, 108, 64, 96, 36,
    24, 8, 54, 12, 6, 48, 42, 80

Further odd tables (threes, fives, sevens and nines)

Page 12

1   Across 12 and 45, down 36 and 15;
    across 54 and 21, down 42 and 27

2   ×3 – 18, 27, 21, 24, 12; ×7 – 42, 63, 49,
    56, 28; ×5 – 30, 45, 35, 40, 20; ×9 – 54,
    81, 63, 72, 36

3   Multiples of 5 – 15, 40, 25; multiples of 7 –
    28, 49, 14; multiples of 9 – 72, 36, 54

Page 13

4   (Clockwise from top) 27, 42, 45; 49, 40,
    36

5   56, 50, 63, 12, 8, 49

6   £40, £42, £72, £18

Page 14

7   2 × 7, 5 × 3 or 3 × 5, 6 × 3 or 2 × 9,
    4 × 5; 7 × 3 or 3 × 7, 8 × 3, 5 × 5, 9 × 3
    or 3 × 9, 4 × 7, 10 × 3 or 6 × 5; 7 × 5 or
    5 × 7, 4 × 9, 8 × 5

8   2, 4, 10, 4, 5, 2, 6, 8, 8, 1, 4, 10

9   Brown – 12, 6, 3, 24; blue – 25, 5, 50, 10,
    40, 20; yellow – 49, 70, 28, 14, 56; green –
    72, 81, 90, 36, 54

Page 15

10 10, 28, 63, 90, 70, 18, 45, 27, 21, 49, 54,
    35, 5, 18, 45, 21, 40, 9, 3, 6, 14, 27, 24, 42,
    63, 7, 15, 50, 72, 30

Further even tables (fours, sixes, eights and tens)

Page 16

1   5 × 4 – red, 1 × 10 – blue; 4 × 8 – red,
    6 × 4 – blue

2   First grid ×8 – 56, 16; ×4 – 28, 8; second
    grid ×8 – 24, 40; ×10 – 30, 50; third grid
    top row 6, 9; ×6 – 54; ×8 – 48

3 20, 24, 28, 30, 32, 54; 12, 24, 36, 40, 60, 72

Page 17

4 3, 4, 5, 6, 7, 8, 2, 8, 5, 2, 6, 5

5 Blue – 6 × 4, 3 × 8, 4 × 6; grey – 9 × 4, 6 × 6; yellow – 4 × 10, 5 × 8, 10 × 4, 5 × 8; black – 9 × 6; green – 10 × 6, 6 × 10; brown – 9 × 8

6 30, 36, 42, 48; 32, 24, 16, 8; 24, 20, 16, 12; 60, 50, 30, 10

Page 18

7 Product

8 4 × 10 and 5 × 8; 3 × 4 and 2 × 6; 9 × 6; 6 × 4, 4 × 6 and 3 × 8

9 £30, 56, 30, 24, 4, £40

Page 19

10 16, 32, 60, 72, 36, 32, 70, 80, 48, 56, 24, 48, 18, 60, 42, 16, 8, 28, 12, 54, 24, 24, 80, 20, 36, 40, 40, 90, 64, 30

Mixed tables (sixes, sevens, eights and nines)

Page 20

1 6 people – 18, 24, 36; 7 people – 21, 28, 42

2 Shade t, w, a, s, l, i, t; sixteen

3 81, 36, 8, 72, 9, true

Page 21

4 45, 54, 72, 81; 35, 28, 21, 14; 48, 56, 64, 72; 12, 18, 24, 36, 42

5 £72, £36, £21, £72, 6, 6

6 Circle red – 12, 30, 42; circle green – 42, 14, 56, 63; circle blue – 27, 63; circle black – 40, 64, 56; 56, 63, 42

Page 22

7 Player A shade 30, 42, 27, 54, 72, 56; Player B shade 42, 54, 72, 63; Player A won

8 9 × 6 and 54; 7 × 7 and 49; 9 × 9 and 81; 6 × 8 and 48; 7 × 9 and 63; 3 × 6 and 18

9 Start, 18, 48, 54, 81, 63, 36, 16, 56, 28, 40, 64, 42, Finish

Page 23

10 36, 72, 60, 72, 81, 32, 49, 56, 48, 56, 28, 48, 18, 42, 42, 16, 8, 63, 45, 54, 54, 24, 80, 63, 36, 90, 64, 70, 40, 30

Mixed tables (twos to twelves)

Page 24

1 7 × 3 – red, 2 × 6 – blue; 9 × 9 – red, 10 × 6 – blue

2 9 × 3 and 27; 7 × 11 and 77; 6 × 4 and 24; 7 × 7 and 49; 9 × 8 and 72; 6 × 2 and 12; 8 × 12 and 96

3 (Clockwise from top) 2 × 12, 3 × 8, 4 × 6, 6 × 4, 8 × 3; 3 × 12, 4 × 9, 9 × 4, 6 × 6

Page 25

4 First grid ×4 – 28, 36, 16; ×6 – 42, 54, 24; ×7 – 49, 63, 28; second grid ×8 – 64, 48, 24; ×3 – 24, 18, 9; ×12 – 96, 72, 36; third grid top row – 5; ×9 – 90, 45; ×11 – 44, 110; ×2 – 8, 10

5 54, 8, 56, 27, 36, 6

6 (Clockwise from top) 24, 56, 60, 108, 56, 32

Page 26

7 42 different facts are possible

8 9, 8, 9, 9, 3, 8, 9, 4, 1, 5, 9, 2

9 (2) 6, 8, 10, 12, 14, 16, 18, 20; (4) 8, 12, 16, 20, 24, 28, 32; (6) 6, 12, 18, 24, 30, 36, 42; (7) 7, 14, 21, 28, 35, 42, 49, 56; (8) 8, 16, 24, 32, 40, 48, 56, 64; (9) 9, 18, 27, 36, 45, 54; (10) 10, 20, 30, 40, 50, 60, 70; (12) 12, 24, 36, 48, 60

Page 27

10 8 × 9 and 6 × 12; 5 × 9 and 9 × 5; 5 × 12 and 10 × 6; 8 × 6 and 4 × 12

11 Across 72 and 24, down 32 and 54; across 42 and 56, down 48 and 49

12 First wall (from top) – 5 × 5, 6 × 7, 9 × 3 or 3 × 9, 8 × 9, 11 × 5 or 5 × 11; second wall (from top) – 40, 110, 21, 18

Page 28

13 Across – (1) 72, (4) 110, (6) 120, (7) 60, (8) 81, (10) 64, (12) 48; down – (2) 21, (3) 20, (5) 100, (6) 108, (9) 16, (11) 44

14 ✔, ✗, ✗, ✔, ✗, ✗, ✔, ✔

15 4, 9, 2, 8, 3

Page 29

16 6, 48, 35, 18, 24, 84, 14, 15, 20, 36, 18, 32, 20, 55, 11, 12, 14, 18, 30, 21, 99, 48, 90, 90, 36, 54, 60, 48, 4, 8, 45, 72, 50, 63, 56, 22, 36, 42, 28, 80, 18, 27, 72, 15, 12, 108, 9, 28

Check your progress

- Shade in the stars on the progress certificate to show how much you did. Shade one star for every ★ you circled in this book.
- If you have shaded fewer than 10 stars go back to the pages where you circled Some ☆ or Most ✦ and try those pages again.
- If you have shaded 10 or more stars you are ready to move on to the next workbook. Well done!

Collins Easy Learning Times Tables Age 7–11 Workbook 3

Progress certificate

to

_____

date

Sevens, nines and elevens		Sixes, eights and twelves		Threes, fives, sevens and nines		Fours, sixes, eights and tens		Sixes, sevens, eights and nines		Twos to twelves		
pages 4–5		pages 8–9	pages 10–11	pages 12–13	pages 14–15	pages 16–17	pages 18–19	pages 20–21	pages 22–23	pages 24–25	pages 26–27	pages 28–29
☆ 1	☆ 2	☆ 3	☆ 4	☆ 5	☆ 6	☆ 7	☆ 8	☆ 9	☆ 10	☆ 11	☆ 12	☆ 13

name _____